MODERN
HAND TO HAND
COMBAT

MODERN
HAND TO HAND
COMBAT

Ancient Samurai Techniques on the Battlefield and in the Street

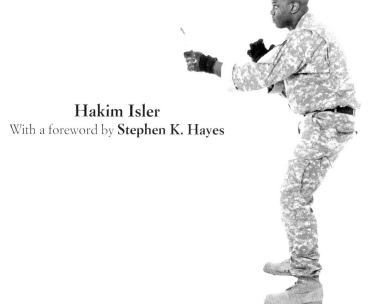

Hakim Isler
With a foreword by **Stephen K. Hayes**

TUTTLE PUBLISHING
Tokyo • Rutland, Vermont • Singapore

Published by Tuttle Publishing, an imprint of Periplus Editions (HK) Ltd.

www.tuttlepublishing.com

Library of Congress Cataloging-in-Publication Data

Isler, Hakim.
  Modern hand-to-hand combat : ancient samurai techniques on the battlefield and in the street / Hakim Isler; with a foreword by Stephen K. Hayes.
     p. cm.
  Includes index.
  ISBN 978-0-8048-4127-6 (hardcover)
1. Hand-to-hand fighting, Oriental. 2. Martial arts. 3. Self-defense. 4. Samurai. I. Title.
  GV1112.I85 2010
  796.815--dc22

                              2010011369

ISBN 978-0-8048-4127-6

Distributed by

North America, Latin America & Europe
Tuttle Publishing
364 Innovation Drive
North Clarendon, VT 05759-9436 U.S.A.
Tel: 1 (802) 773-8930; Fax: 1 (802) 773-6993
info@tuttlepublishing.com
www.tuttlepublishing.com

Asia Pacific
Berkeley Books Pte. Ltd.
61 Tai Seng Avenue #02-12
Singapore 534167
Tel: (65) 6280-1330; Fax: (65) 6280-6290
inquiries@periplus.com.sg
www.periplus.com

Japan
Tuttle Publishing
Yaekari Building, 3rd Floor
5-4-12 Osaki
Shinagawa-ku
Tokyo 141 0032
Tel: (81) 3 5437-0171; Fax: (81) 3 5437-0755
tuttle-sales@gol.com

14 13 12 11 10   10 9 8 7 6 5 4 3 2 1

Printed in Singapore

TABLE OF CONTENTS

DISCLAIMER

Warning! Some of the topics discussed in this book might be seen as a challenge or an attempt to degrade other systems in the combative community. It is not my intention to single out any one system or invalidate it. If anything, I wish to add another aspect of thinking to the saturated field of military combatives, and hopefully inspire the reader toward another level of combat proficiency.

Important notice: Whilst every effort has been made to ensure that the content of this book is as safe and technically accurate as possible, neither the author nor the publishers can accept responsibility for any injury or loss sustained as a result of the use of this material. It is the responsibility of the individual to ensure that they are fit to participate and they should seek medical advice from a qualified professional where appropriate.

FOREWORD

When I first heard about the Battlefield Proximity Combat system, created by my friend and student Hakim Isler, I wondered why such a system was needed. I thought surely someone has done this before. It seems like common sense that if you are going to send a combat soldier, who is wearing up to a hundred pounds of gear, weapons, and armor into battle, you would want to train him or her in a combat system that focused on how to win a fight for life on the battlefield.

The more I spoke with Hakim and other military friends about training for hand-to-hand survival in battle, the more surprised I became. It turns out that very little, if any, time and attention is given to providing realistic pragmatic training in preparing the soldier's body, intellect, and spirit on how to achieve victory in those admittedly rare occasions when the battle degenerates down to an eye-to-eye struggle between determined adversaries.

I am aware that some branches of the United States military offer forms of spirit-building training based on sport grappling or sport boxing. Of course, these are by nature spirit-builders only, intended to foster fighting grit in young soldiers as opposed to teaching them what to do to survive the horror of a murderous assault. Spirit-building practice is carried out in light training clothes and not actual battle gear. Techniques taught are based on two individuals, each struggling for the submission of the other, and this does not address the practical techniques needed to preserve lives in actual combat. Spirit-building certainly has a valuable place in the education of young soldiers, but it can in no way replace honest preparation in how to avoid the kind of body and mind lock-up that happens in real battles and could result in death.

As an avid student of Japanese cultural and military history, and an apprentice to the ninja grandmaster in Japan in the 1970s, I have taken the ancient traditions, combat strategies, and philosophies of Japan's ninja warriors and adapted them for use in the very different thinking West. Obviously, combat in 21st century America is different from that of the 1500s Japan, so technologies of engagement must also change. Nonetheless, the principles and philosophies are still highly valid and can be adapted. Yes, I still teach historical techniques to those interested, but unlike those traditionalists who hold to antiquated rigidity of form and structure, I realize that an honest and realistic update has to evolve…and here it is in Hakim's book.

As you read and re-read Hakim's book, ask yourself critical questions as you move from chapter to chapter.

How prepared am I to win in a horrific unpredictable battle clash?

How much do I know about how the body and brain operates under the surge of stress chemicals released in a dire survival conditions?

How much have I prepared for life saving combat through honest realistic training beyond the manly fun of wrestling a fellow soldier?

How ready am I to let go of the comfort of my previous beliefs and face the chilling prospect of rebuilding my combat preparedness in a whole new and different way?

I believe in Hakim Isler, and I believe in the system he has built based on our training together in Ohio and his life-saving experiences in the sands of the Mideast. Enjoy Hakim's book. Learn and grow.

Stephen K. Hayes
Founder, Kasumi-An To-Shin Do Ninja Martial Arts
Black Belt Hall of Fame
Author of Tuttle book, *The Ninja and Their Secret Fighting Art*

❂   ❂   ❂   ❂   ❂

As a member of the Special Operations community for 12 years, I have commanded several unique organizations with a variety of missions. Over the years I have come to realize that combative training is a key ingredient in the making of a Special Ops individual. The Special Operations community employs a variety of combative training systems. The recent evolution of the Battlefield Proximity Combat system captures the essence of all the others, but incorporates new techniques against evolving threats in the 21st century. I have personally observed Hakim Isler teach his system to my soldiers, who were operating in the toughest parts of Ramadi, Iraq. The confidence with which these soldiers were able to operate on the forward edge of the battlefield always paid dividends.

LTC Michael Layrisson, U.S. Army

chapter 1

JOURNEY TO CREATION

I t was 6 a.m. as we formed up for physical fitness training (PT) at Fort Bragg, North Carolina. Orders for our PT uniform that day was that we were to wear battle dress uniforms (BDUs) and boots. The mood that day was a somber one, because we figured that there would be a long log run or some other difficult team building event, undoubtedly raising the "suck factor" of our lives. When cadre appeared, I remember getting that all too familiar feeling of anxiety that comes from finding out what was to come. We were given the eight commands necessary to get us ready to perform PT, and then we were informed that we would be conducting combative training.

I was 25 at the time and a newbie to the Army. However, since I was 8 years old, I had been studying the martial arts, so I had 17 years of experience by that point. You can imagine the my enthusiasm that morning after finding out that we would be studying combatives. Previously, I had only received a small block of instruction in basic training at Fort Benning. The training was not very impressive, but it wasn't supposed to be. It seemed that the primary focus was to instill a fighting spirit in myself and the other soldiers. Now that I stood on the grass of "The Home of Special Operations," I knew I would be learning things that would impress me.

As we began, I immediately felt like I had been thrust into a selection phase of a special school rather than a combatives class. For the next 40 minutes, we were ordered to perform a series of physical exercises designed to completely diminish our strength and energy. Although the others did not understand how this was related to combatives, I knew what was happening. I knew the cadre wanted us to be at a point of muscle failure so that when we were taught the techniques we couldn't rely solely on our physical strength. With fatigue gripping our bodies, we'd really have to mentally focus to accomplish the techniques and achieve the desired results. I had seen this tactic used in several schools before, but never at such an early stage. I certainly thought that the techniques I was going to learn would blow my mind.

After the "smoke session" (an extremely high-paced and demanding workout) was over, we formed a circle around the cadre. Finally, the cadre members started to demonstrate the techniques that we would be working on for the remainder of our PT time. As they started the demonstration, my mouth almost dropped to the floor. I wasn't amazed at all. On the contrary, I was shocked. What I saw was very rigid, unrealistic, and unstable. The rigidity wasn't much of a problem in my mind; I expected some of this, because it is sometimes easier to convey combatives this way when teaching to a crowd of people. The main problems were the unrealistic and hypocritical aspects of the techniques.

What I mean by *unrealistic* is that we spent our first 40 minutes of training being worn down so that we could not use strength, only to then learn techniques that only worked by using a great deal of strength. The cadre members were constantly yelling at the trainees to "pull harder, hit harder, or kick harder" when a technique wasn't working. In my mind, I searched for a way to defend their methods. I told myself that they were just trying to instill a fighting spirit in us. But the fact is that they were yelling at people who couldn't

perform due to their fatigue. It made me wonder. In truth, it wasn't spirit that was the problem; the techniques required too much energy and strength to be correctly performed.

So why did we start to succeed when we were yelled at? Well, no one wanted to hyperextend his or her arm because they were trying to be a successful attacker. So, what we started doing was taking it easy for the next attack or loosening our grip so that the defense could succeed.

Here's another point: Let's assume that both Soldier A and Soldier B are exhausted during a combative drill. Now, let's have Soldier A attack Soldier B. If Soldier B can't defend against Soldier A's attack when exhausted, how is Soldier B going to successfully defend against a fresh and ready opponent? How can Soldier B hope to succeed, regardless of whatever sound combative technique he or she may be employing, if Soldier B simply cannot operate at full potential?

Another aspect I found unrealistic was that we were doing things like simulating arm breaks, rib breaks, and kicks to the face with combat boots, sometimes all in the same technique. What was our opponent doing as we performed our techniques? Unfortunately, more often than not, they were staring off into space. There was no reality-based consideration for the reaction of an attacker getting his or her arm or ribs broken, or being kicked in the face. Initially, I thought this was because we were in the beginning phase of our combative training. I had taught static training to beginners before, where there's less of a consideration for "real" reactions during combat. However, as the classes continued, the consideration for reactions was never covered.

Along with this lack of consideration for realistic reaction was what I call the "Action Movie Syndrome." This happens when people put too many movements into a technique set. Thus, you break an arm, then a rib, then strike the face, then the neck, and then have a cup of coffee before the guy hits the ground. Wow! It all looks very cool, but it is not efficient or effective—except maybe in a movie-generated situation. I don't like to say that certain things or techniques will "never" work; you can, after all, cut a steak with a fork, but it's going to be difficult. In a real fight, if you break an opponent's arm, he or she now has a big problem. Even if he or she can continue to fight with one arm down, he or she would almost have to be a superhero. Or, this person would have to be extremely high on some substance to ignore the painful reality of a broken arm!

Furthermore, when you break someone's arm, that person isn't just going to stand there. You can bank on the fact that the attacker's body dynamic is going to change. But what does that mean? Well, it might mean that the "Five-Combo Hurricane Kick" you were planning next won't work that well.

Another major flaw I noticed as our combatives training continued was that everything was done with our legs nearly straight. The result was poor balance, with soldiers falling all over the place. There was no mention of bending one's knees and getting low to the ground as a way to gain stability and maintain a better center of gravity. There was no mention that tall, straight legs meant lack of balance and weak technique. Maybe it was because we were just supposed to learn the basics; this was just an introductory course in combative training.

Well, guess what? The things I am talking about *are* the basics, and to neglect them at the beginning means bigger problems down the line.

Even though I felt so many things were a little off about what was being taught, I still had no real desire to work toward making it better. Although I'd already written a book and created a curriculum for a self-protection art, I felt I didn't have enough knowledge on the needs of the military to create my own comprehensive combatives system. Besides, my focus was on completing my military training. It really wasn't until I made it to my unit, linked up with my team, and began training to deploy to Iraq that I started learning what service members would really need on the battlefield.

My first revelation came when I had to put my armor on and go out on a mock patrol. I remember feeling how awkward and heavy my armor was, and I wasn't even carrying ammo yet. Because I had gone to bodyguard school before the Army, I was well versed in role-playing situations. I immediately started thinking about how would I fight with all this equipment on my person. Needless to say, the answers didn't come from anything I was taught by that cadre on that early morning or the days that followed. The moves were too quick, unstable, required too much energy for what I was wearing.

I started thinking about the last martial arts system I learned, which I studied for five years before joining the Army. Its principles and philosophies came from an ancient Japanese lineage where people often fought wearing heavy armor. I began to think more about the relationship between what I was wearing and what the samurai wore on the battlefields of Japan. During training, I was told that I would spend at least fifty percent of my time in this uniform while I was in Iraq. So why, then, didn't my training cover close-quarters hand-to-hand combat with this uniform? I thought more about those ancient principles and wondered if I could create a system based on them. After all, in both concept and reality, protective armor has transcended the span of time. Could those ancient combat principles transcend as well? The samurai were masters at warfare, could their teachings still be useful on today's battlefield?

I started to tinker with this concept and began developing several techniques. Then one day, I found myself talking with a staff sergeant from my unit who had spent most of his Army career on the judo team—until he came to our unit. I told him what I was doing and he thought it was a great idea. He said he had talked to the First Sergeant and was going to be giving a ground fighting class for PT on Thursdays. He asked if I would be willing to demonstrate some of my newly developed techniques, because he felt it was geared more towards what we would really face on the battlefield.

I was elated, as you can imagine, but I had no official curriculum, so I told him I wasn't sure if I was ready. He talked me into giving it a try, and I spent the next few days organizing my notes and techniques. When Thursday rolled around, we had, according to the participants, "a good class that made a lot of sense." To some, my theories were revolutionary, further encouraging me to believe that maybe I really was onto something. I taught a few more classes before my unit scrapped the Thursday combative class to make room for other necessary training for deployment. However, I received enough positive feedback that I kept working on the curriculum.

Battlefield Proximity Combat (B.P.C.) seemed to grow from infancy to adulthood during my time in Iraq. It was on the ground there that I gained personal experience and had conversations with others about the battlefield and what was needed. In addition, I was able to conduct B.P.C. classes during my downtime at the gym. Class availability was mission dependent, but even when I couldn't make it, the other practitioners would run their own classes, working on the material I taught in prior classes. The fact that they were capable of doing this in such a short time, again, proved to me that I was on the right track. During my 15-month tour, I trained a number of classes filled with men and women of the Army, Marines, and the Navy, as well as military contractors. It was fun and inspiring work.

This book is also a result of the time that I spent fighting and training in the desert. Mind you, I don't believe that B.P.C. is the "ultimate authority" of all combative systems. But, it can be a great introduction to combatives, or a great addition to current or future training. I believe that everything—even the system I began learning on that early morning—has some value. Knowledge is the first step towards strength; the second step is its application.

chapter 2

LESSONS FROM THE PAST

TRANSCENDING TIME

A strong study of the past will help us make better decisions in the future.

One of America's strengths is its ability to integrate ideas from various sources and influences to accomplish our objectives. However, when we don't have a proper understanding of an idea then its integration won't lead to success in achieving our goals. Combatives are no different.

There has been so much misuse and general misconception of the martial arts systems that are being taught for hand-to-hand combat on the battlefield. This misconception, I feel, comes from not properly assessing the needs of a modern fighting force resulting in improper principles and tactics.

I believe that there is no need to completely reinvent the wheel. There once existed a warrior and fighting force that had many similarities to the modern American fighting force: samurai warriors. In many ways, today's military service member can be perceived as a modern samurai. Similarities range from the advanced capabilities of service members to a similarity in values/virtues:

Army: 7 Values	Samurai: 7 Virtues
Loyalty	Rectitude – (strong moral integrity)
Duty	Courage
Respect	Benevolence – (an inclination to be kind)
Selfless service	Respect
Honor	Honesty
Integrity	Honor
Personal courage	Loyalty

The virtues expected of the U.S. soldier bears a remarkable resemblance to those of a samurai warrior. The modern soldier can adapt more than these martial virtues, it's from the samurai that an effective, efficient, and simple means of armored hand-to-hand combat can be adapted for today's battlefield.

Misconceiving the Battle

There is a thriving misconception in America's martial arts community that many of the older martial arts systems (which are still studied today) were created as a response to battlefield conditions and, thus, have been battlefield tested. Therefore, to those who teach these systems to the military, it makes perfect sense that these arts are appropriate for fighting in a modern battlefield environment. The truth is that many of these martial arts systems came from a time and place where people were not encumbered by the modern American warfighter's weaknesses, nor endowed with their strengths in battle.

In regards to most of the systems that originated in Japan, which are either taught in America or are the foundation of American systems, their origins probably reach back to the start of the peaceful era of Japan's history: the Edo Era, which began around 1603. This eventually transitioned into the peaceful era known as the Meiji restoration, which started in 1868. Most martial art systems studied today originated during the Meiji restoration. Martial arts born during this period were called *budo* ("martial way/path"), but are now called *gendai budo* ("modern martial way/path"). Because they were spawned during peace, these martial arts focused more on the inner aspects of the practitioner than they did on battlefield preparedness and application. Thus, these arts— though tested in competitions and in other fashions—were not necessarily tested on the battlefield. Some of the martial arts born during the Meiji Era include judo, kendo, iaido, aikido, and kempo.

Before this peaceful era, there was a definitive militaristic interest placed on martial systems. Because the periods before the Edo Era and Meiji Era were riddled with war, the emphasis on battlefield combat was of utmost importance. The period that spawned the creation of many of these battlefield systems was called the *Sengoku Jidai* (Period of the Warring States), which lasted approximately from the mid-1400s to 1573. These systems are known today as *koryu bujutsu* (old tradition martial techniques). However, during the Warring State Period they were simply called *bujutsu* (martial techniques).

For the samurai, fighting in close-quarters hand-to-hand combat was viewed as honorable, and sometimes even preferred, therefore, close-combat methods for the battlefield were given great emphasis. Understanding that close quarter fighting would occur while wearing armor, these systems would extensively cover fighting with weapons and grappling while wearing heavy body armor. These armed and unarmed combat methods of fighting while armored had many names, such as: *Koshi no Mawari*, *Katchu Bujutsu*, *Yoroi Kumiuchi*, *Yotsugumi*, and *Kogusoku*.

Protecting the Body

The samurai wore many different types of armor, depending on the time period and construction. However, two main styles primarily stood apart from the rest: the *O-yoroi* and the *Domaru*. The *O-yoroi* ("great/big armor") was used primarily for mounted cavalry due to its weight. This armor was worn only by the upper class and higher-ranking samurai.

The *Domaru* ("around the body") was lighter and, therefore, worn primarily by the infantry. When reading about these two styles of armor, one who has stepped foot on the modern day battlefield will be reminded of the difference between armor worn while mounted in the turret gunner's seat and the armor worn by the dismounted service member. In Iraq, generally, the turret gunner had to wear more armor because of his greater risk of exposure. Snipers and improvised explosive devices (I.E.D.s) caused many casualties, due to the exposure of this position. The answer was to provide more personal armor for the turret gunner. Dismounted individuals, although more exposed, have to move on foot while carrying heavy equipment. Thus, they sometimes wore less armor to reduce or balance out the weight on their bodies and maintain some level of agility while conducting urban operations.

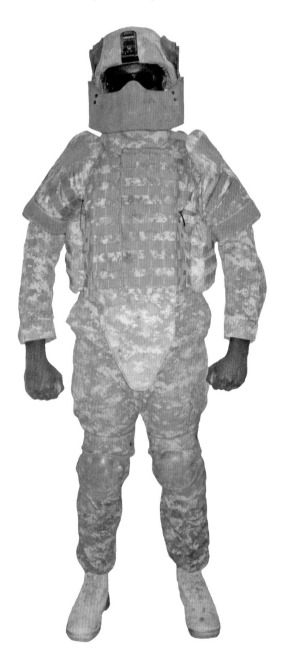

Armor Comparison

For its time, samurai armor was very advanced in its protective nature and design. As stated earlier, improvements were constantly being made as samurai returning from the battlefield provided information on changes that could enhance their armor's effectiveness, as well as information gained from other cultures. Through similar trial and error, we are learning and improving our armor in the same way the samurai did so long ago. The armor worn by today's U.S. military not only bears great resemblance in design and function to the samurai's, but the weight of the armor is also similar. Samurai armor could weigh 60 pounds and up; the modern U.S. service member's armor and full combat kit also starts at 60 pounds and proceeds upward. As a visual testament to this fact, I have provided a comparison of modern Army armor to samurai armor in function and design.

Kabuto (Samurai)

The *kabuto* was the helmet of the samurai. One of the names for the example shown here was *suji-bachi kabuto* (ribbed bowl helmet), which protected the samurai's head from blunt trauma injuries, as well as helping to deflect projectiles and bladed weapons. Not shown here is the helmet's U-shaped neck guard, or the *shikoro*, which was a series of scales that hung from the helmet's rim.

Ballistic Helmet (Army)

The modern military ballistic helmet, also known as the "Mitch" helmet, weighs about 3.5 lbs and can protect the head from blunt trauma, fragmentation, etc.

Mempo (Samurai)

This facemask was used to protect the face and add to the fierceness of a samurai's character. It was also called the *men yori,* which meaning "face armor." It often came with a throat protector, sometimes referred to as the *nodawa.*

Rotational Maxillofacial Shield kit (Army)

This experimental facemask arrived in Iraq for testing by certain units some time in early to mid-2007. Its function was to provide protection from shrapnel and bullet fragmentation.

Nodawa (Samurai)

Hanging under, and most often attached to, the *men yoroi* (face armor) was a piece of armor that protected the neck and throat of a samurai. This protector, often called the *nodawa,* could also have been named *eriwa* or *guruwa.* Its primary function was to protect the neck from piercing and slashing during combat.

Throat Protector (Army)

This piece of protective gear is part of the Interceptor Body Armor (I.B.A.), and is used to protect the neck from small fragments and shrapnel from explosions or debris from bullets impacting surrounding objects. It can also offer some protection for the neck from weapons such as knives or empty-handed strikes.

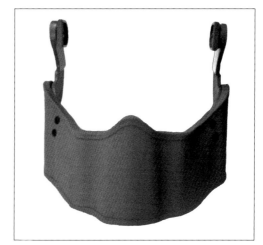

Do (Samurai)

The *do* (upper body armor) protected the samurai's torso. Depending on the time period, it could have been constructed of scales, lamellar, or a full plate. It would serve to protect against stabs, slashes, and, in some instances, projectile deflection.

I.B.A - Interceptor Body Armor (Army)

The Interceptor Body Armor, also known as the Individual Body Armor (shown here with the side ballistic inserts), is worn to protect the torso of the body. Along with enhanced small-arms protective inserts, this body armor can protect a service member from an array of battlefield dangers that can cause bodily damage.

Sode (Samurai)

The *sode* was the piece of the samurai's armor that protected his shoulder and upper arm. It normally hung over the shoulder to the elbow. Normally worn on both arms, these "many shields" (as some would call them) helped protect from slashes and stabs, and, in some instances, would deflect projectile weapons.

Deltoid Upper Arm Protector (Army)

The deltoid upper arm protector was fielded primarily as a means to help protect soldiers from shrapnel passing through the outside of the upper arm and into their torso. It attaches to the I.B.A and then straps under the arm.

Tekko (Samurai)

The *tekko* was the piece of the Samurai's armor that protected his hands. It normally covered the back of the hand from the wrist to the middle knuckles. The *tekko* helped protect from the hands from cuts and abrasions and was, in some instances, used in strikes.

Tactical Gloves (Army)

Tactical gloves are used primarily to protect the hands from cuts and abrasions, as well as structural damage that could be sustained during a struggle. If they are made of fire retardant materials they can reduce fire related injuries.

Japanese Armor

American Armor

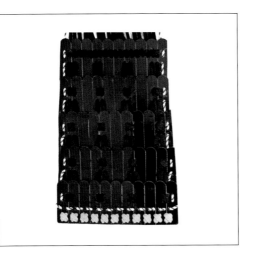 

Kusazuri (Samurai)

The *kusazuri* protected the samurai's upper thighs and groin area from slashes. Several of these plates would hang from the *do* and cover the upper front and back portion of the thighs.

Groin Protector (Army)

This piece of protective gear is worn to protect the groin area from shrapnel and other indirect projectile damage.

Some of these pieces were optional. For the samurai, if you were from the lower classes you would have worn cheaper, lighter armor. If you are a modern military member, depending on your command, availability, and whether you are mounted or dismounted, certain pieces of your armor would or would not be worn. However, no matter what the uniform, the likeness of the samurai armor to the modern day service member's battlefield armor is uncanny. It seems that, even today, we are following an unspoken standard for body armor. This is not to say that the Japanese were the only culture to create armor following this standard—Europeans had similar armor. However, the point of this section is to show why the *bujutsu* principles of hand-to-hand close-quarters armored combat that the samurai used during their time would serve well as the foundation for a combatives system for the modern day armored warrior or, as I like to say, the modern samurai.

Chapter 3

B.P.C. PHILOSOPHY

As to methods there may be a million and then some, but principles are few.
The man who grasps principles can successfully select his own methods. The
man who tries methods, ignoring principles, is sure to have trouble.

-Ralph Waldo Emerson

WHAT IS B.P.C.?

B.P.C. is a newly evolved combative system addressing the needs of the American military as they face the budding threat of the 21st Century. The focuses of B.P.C.'s curriculum are operational realism; degradation of combative proximities and combative capabilities; and escalation of force. B.P.C. finds most of its philosophy rooted in ancient Japanese battlefield combative principles. There is special emphasis placed on samurai close-quarters combative principles while in armor. Due to the similarities between samurai armor and modern battlefield personal combat equipment, these principles find a new calling and a new era of usability.

It is no secret that, in combat, you always want to have better positioning, overwhelming odds, overwhelming fire power, and the element of surprise. However, this is not always the reality of the war zone. Sometimes, service members find themselves without any of these things in a one-on-one encounter with the enemy. To some, this is called the worst-case scenario and its father is Murphy, last name Law. B.P.C. preparation makes these worst-case scenarios not that bad.

Why Combatives?

During my time in the military, I have often heard the common question: "Why do I need combatives if I have a gun? If it comes down to protecting myself, I'm just going to shoot my opponent." As someone coming from the Special Ops community, I'd say: "That's damn right—if I'm in a firefight." If only the world of a service member were that simple all the time. A direct action mission may be to move in, kill everything in sight, and exfiltrate, but this is seldom the actual chain of events. Even then, there are times where one will have to use more than bullets, due to malfunctions, lack of ammo, need for silence, etc. Throughout the military there is a conglomerate of situations, scenarios, and missions in which service members have to carefully know the rules of engagement for their operational environments. These rules of engagement instigate the need for training in each aspect of the use of force, based on the severity and danger of the situation. Training should not just cover the policies regarding escalation of force. Soldiers also need to be trained on how to properly execute defensive or offensive tactics based on an escalating situation. They need to understand the degradation of battlefield proximities and combative capabilities, and to understand operational realism. Without a proper repertoire of options and skills to use in select situations, a service member could possibly overreact, or fail to react in an efficient or effective way.

Normally, in a combat zone, you will have a weapon. But weapons, and the people who carry them, are not always that reliable. In Iraq, it became quickly apparent that you weren't always going to be in optimal situations. That 9mm Beretta that had been passed around numerous times might have a magazine that gets stuck and malfunctions.

I remember talking to a soldier who said combatives were useless. He would rather have had more shooting training, which he felt was not emphasized enough, because he had only been to eight shooting ranges in the three years that he was in the Army (spending maybe 30-40 minutes shooting each time). He also said that most of his shooting training was stationary and in the prone position.

I agreed with the idea of more shooting practice, but I also said that, as combat soldiers, it is our job to be complete warriors, not just half of one. Teaching a soldier how to shoot a rifle but not how to shoot his pistol is not properly preparing him; to teach him how to convoy but not how to foot patrol is no good; to teach him how to shoot stationary but not how to bound and overwatch only teaches him half of what is needed. The Army learned long ago that training all soldiers in first aid helped raise the probability of wounded casualties surviving in combat. Instead of waiting for a combat medic to arrive on the scene, any battle buddy can provide some aid to the wounded. Chances of survival for everyone in a unit are based on everyone's training as a complete soldier.

In the Army FM 7-1, the field manual for Battle Focused Training, it states "Units should train in peacetime as they will fight in war. Peacetime training should replicate battlefield conditions." So the question is: Isn't it possible for a service member to close with and meet the enemy in a close-quarters hand-to-hand combat altercation? If the answer is "yes," which it is, then the next question is: Has that service member been effectively trained to meet that enemy in close-quarters hand-to-hand combat in armor, and on all other levels in a way that will lead to success? B.P.C. is a necessary part in the development of a complete warfighter.

chapter 4
FOCUSES OF B.P.C. TRAINING

UNDERSTANDING ESCALATION OF FORCE

L et's face it, if a service member has to kill someone in hand-to-hand combat, either he or she has a high-speed Military Occupational Specialty (M.O.S. – job or job designator) or Murphy (as in Murphy's Law) has given him or her a good kick in the buttocks. However, going back to my original point, this is rarely the overall common experience of service members. Normally, service members find themselves in escalating situations. When I was in Iraq, my friend and I would be sitting at a combat outpost talking and then, suddenly, a hail of weapons fire would erupt. Not all escalation of force is this extreme, but it happens.

During this same incident, this Marine (on the right), who was out in the open at the time, fell in a mud pit while running for cover from indirect rifle fire. Needless to say his weapon would have to undergo a thorough cleaning to ensure 100 percent functionality. However, imagine the problems he might have faced if he had to go into a close quarters battle with his weapon, directly following his mud bath.

This type of escalation is more often the rule than the exception. During one of my several encounters while in Iraq, my team and I were sitting at a combat outpost preparing for a mission that we were to take part in that night. Suddenly the outpost was under fireattack as a part of a coordinated attack on multiple locations by the insurgents. My team and I geared up and went to the roof to provide support. Once onto the roof we separated and went to help out on different sides of the building. On my side of the building, a US sniper directed me to watch a wall from where he believed we had been taking fire, while he moved to another location to provide long range over-watch. No sooner had he left when a man emerged from behind the wall. Fortunately for him he was not carrying a weapon. However, we knew that often times the insurgent forces would engage us from cover and when they were out of ammo they would throw away their weapons and emerge looking like your everyday citizen. This made it hard to act because you never knew if the person was an innocent citizen caught in the crossfire or the enemy himself. This same issue was very daunting when on a mission in the community because you never new who you were truly dealing with. One moment you could be in a harmless face-to-face meeting and the next minute you could be in a struggle that may call for the use of a weapon or it may call for a hands-on struggle resulting in a detaining situation. An inappropriate reaction to any one of these situations could create more damage to the war effort than one could imagine. Unpredictable escalation is always looming and on today's battlefield, and a rifle is not and cannot be the answer, especially if it malfunctions.

One of the greatest benefits of training a service member on how to handle escalating situations is that it raises their confidence level. When provided with the proper tools, knowledge, and discretion, the service member becomes empowered, knowing that he or she has options that have been provided through this training. This helps alleviate some of the stress, and prevents overreaction (or lack of action) due to the service member feeling incapable of making a policy-supported response to an action taken by someone in his or her area of operation.

When I was in Iraq, there were times my team and I would have a medical assistance mission. Sometimes the people would get very anxious, get out of line, and try to push through or sneak past.

In this situation, it would be inappropriate for a team member to pull out an extendable baton and beat the person, or draw down on the person with a weapon. However, something had to be done to establish control and dominance. If control wasn't established, the line would begin stampeding forward, trying to overwhelm us. This type of situation can be very intimidating and events could quickly turn from giving aid for common maladies to giving aid for soldier-inflicted wounds. However, in my personal situation, a simple control technique effectively accomplished what screaming and yelling by my comrades could not accomplish. Overreaction can destroy developed trust and positive psychological perception, as well as military careers.

Degradation of Proximities and Capabilities

In addition to having options in the realm of escalating force, knowing how to manipulate and improvise during the degradation of combative proximities and combative capabilities is also very important. Once force has been escalated, or once a situation that started as distant combat becomes close quarter combat, the employment of all weapons to their full capacity is important. During my training as a soldier, I felt that this was not focused on enough. If a soldier runs out of ammo, or his pistol or rifle malfunctions, can he or she effectively and efficiently still use it as a blunt trauma weapon? If not, can he or she effectively and efficiently use a knife, a baton, stick, and, finally, bare hands? This type of training brings a service member much closer to completion as a warfighter. It also continues to nurture the service member's confidence level.

Some combative systems don't put enough emphasis (or none at all) on using all weapons to their fullest capacity. I believe that this is partially due to two flaws in the development of these systems. The first is a lack of true understanding in the degradation of combat proximities and combative capabilities; the second is the lack of proper attention to operational realism.

Just as an example, during the heat of battle it is very easy to expend all the rounds in a magazine. Even when I've been at the shooting range, I sometimes lost track of how many shots I had fired. In some schools and training academies, they say it is important to keep track of the shot count, but this is easier said than done. One can easily imagine a situation where, in the heat of a firefight while shooting, moving, and communicating, one could move to a new position and unexpectedly come face-to-face with an aggressor. However, when the soldier raises his or her weapon and pulls the trigger, nothing happens. The weapon is either out of ammo or jammed. What now? Does the soldier (a) begin reloading the weapon; (b) pretend he or she has ammo and try to take the aggressor prisoner; (c) assault through the target using his rifle as a blunt trauma weapon, incapacitate his opponent, then reload, or apply S.P.O.R.T.S (slap, pull, observe, release, tap, squeeze), which is a trained method for clearing a M16 or a M4 rifle; or (d) deploy a secondary weapon and incapacitate the adversary?

I'd say the correct answers are (c) and (d). In close-quarter proximity, before the aggressor has time to realize that your weapon isn't working, use that moment of hesitation to your advantage. Situations like this should be looked at when running through the plethora of worst-case scenarios, based on operational realism.

Operational Creation Based on Operational Realism

Nowadays, there is a craze for reality-based martial arts. In the effort to create a reality-based martial art, one needs to realize that not everyone's reality is the same. All military combative systems stem from either a primary martial art system or a culmination of many different martial arts systems. Usually what happens is that someone, like me, looks at their system and picks a set of techniques that they think are relevant to an operational situation. There is no problem with this, and I have seen some great systems in my experience with military combatives. However, for every great thing I've seen, my comrades and I have also seen things that are irrelevant or impractical to our operational environment.

Reasons for this lack of practicality vary. Some of those who create new combative systems don't always follow the same guidelines. Or, they don't share the same motivation for creating these systems as those who have created systems in the past. In past centuries, during the creation of some of the older, well known martial art systems, a person or group of people would essentially conduct a threat assessment of their enemies. This assessment would address the enemy's mindset, strengths, weaknesses, attack patterns, etc. This group would then take a look at its physical needs and capabilities, as well as its technology. Once this information was gathered, the group would begin designing its martial art system. After a rough draft of the system was hammered out, the system would then enter a testing phase, in which these combative theories were put into practice on the field of battle. Through trial, error, and time, these arts evolved and techniques were added or removed. Granted, I am no historian, and this is definitely not how every martial art system started, but I do believe this is a logical and accurate portrayal of the creation of a typical martial art.

Looking again at our world today, there are so many martial arts systems that I won't even pretend to be familiar with every one. However, I will say that there are very few completely new martial arts systems. What I mean by

this is that most martial art systems today are personalized versions of older systems. Typically, a student becomes a teacher, and when he or she teaches, they create a change or evolution in the art based consciously or subconsciously on his or her own personal strengths, weaknesses, and personality. Therefore, there are many arts with similar, or even identical, historical origins. I believe some of these people don't know, forget, or don't properly address the origins of their art, which prevents them from properly applying it to modern relevant situations. Thus, you have people teaching karate techniques to women for self-defense and guys teaching ground fighting to infantry soldiers. No disrespect intended to either karate or ground fighting. I like all martial arts and think each one definitely has their place.

Personally, I love ground fighting. Yet, I've been with the infantry in Ramadi, and running from house to house wearing full combat equipment isn't fun.

But even less fun than running around with a full kit on is falling and getting up or rolling around with a full kit on. Every time I ever practiced ground fighting in the military I only wore a battle dress uniform or an Army combat uniform, which is not very realistic when compared to what I was going to face in Iraq.

It wasn't until I started writing the B.P.C. curriculum that I started training with I.B.A., and the difference was immediately obvious. Believe me, if you have a full kit on and are ground fighting against a guy with no I.B.A., you will quickly see who has the advantage. For an embassy guard or military police (M.P.) in garrison or detainee facility, ground fighting will be more effective and more likely. But this is not the case on today's battlefield.

I remember at the start of a B.P.C. class in Iraq, a gentleman asked when we would start ground fighting. I replied that we would be ground fighting, but that it might not be what the class participants were used to practicing.

"What do you mean by that?" the questioner pressed.

"Well, we ground fight with one guy in I.B.A., one without, and only long enough for someone to pull out a blade and stab the other or long enough for the service member to get to a position of advantage," I answered. (You can refer to the chapter on battlefield ground combat [B.G.C.] for more about B.P.C.'s version of ground fighting.)

Needless to say, the look on his face was priceless. "Wow!" was his response, then he turned and walked out of the class.

The truth is that everything has its place, but in finding that place, one has to truly look at the operational environment, and the operational realism needed for the place of operation. Just because some guy walks into a ring and beats up a hundred guys with a "Flying Dragon Tail Hook Kick," doesn't mean that it will work in full combat gear in the war-torn streets of the modern urban battlefield.

I remember asking a Navy SEAL, whom I met in the gym before his ground fighting classes began, what he thought about the combatives training he experienced as a SEAL. I asked him to name some good and bad points. He didn't have much to say on the positive side. As we talked about what I was doing and what he was doing, it became apparent that he was a fan of mixed martial arts (MMA) competitions. He knew the names of all the major fighters, as well as their histories, abilities, and the various organizations governing the then-emerging MMA community.

Eventually, we came to a point in the conversation where he said he was unimpressed by all the nonsense out there, especially in the military. His next words, though, blew my mind. He said: "There are so many guys out there saying this and that about who they are, what they can do, and that their system is the best. However, I feel if they really want to see or prove that their system is the best they should go into the ring and test their skills."

"Wow!" I thought. How can anyone test a system designed for the battlefield in the ring? When the ring has a different set of rules? Even if the ring didn't have rules, who would test a military combatives system's lethality in a ring? Maybe a military's non-lethal techniques could be tested in a ring. Again, not that I am an historian, but I can't think of too many times in history that someone created a technique or tactic for the battlefield and then decided they would test it in a competition.

There have been such things as death matches throughout history, but, overall, systems and methods created for the battlefield—whether tactics, techniques, or weaponry—found their true test on the battlefield. The SEAL's statement proved to me that the American combative society has grown overly infatuated with, and in some ways misguided by, the combat competitive entertainment of MMA. Muhammad Ali could probably kick my butt in a boxing match, dancing and punching me into oblivion. But if I put a full combat kit on him, ran him through a Cordon and Search, then told him to box to the death with a person who is not exhausted while encumbered by his body armor, what do you think would happen? Regardless, when a Navy SEAL, who is trained to kill, talks to you about proving battlefield techniques in a

Standard combat-outpost uniform

Standard combat uniform

There are two main possibilities when it comes to uniforms in the battlefield. Depending on branch of service, comfort, and duty, there could be slight variations to these uniforms. When considering creation based on operational realism, combatives should encompass training in both uniforms.

competitive arena, it proves how easy it is for one to misunderstand the importance of operational realism.

It's not unusual for people to make the mistake of not properly understanding the origin of a martial art. Looking at the origin of a martial art provides an understanding of the operational needs of those who created it. In this way, a practitioner can design a system that is based on thorough, analytical comparisons, which allows for the transfer of effective methods fitting the operational needs of the people who will be implementing it in a realistic setting.

For example, if a martial art was created by a people who were very poor and had no high-tech weaponry or armor, yet their enemy had the opposite capabilities (wealth, high-tech

It was mandatory for even Santa to carry a pistol in Ramadi

weaponry, and armor), naturally their weapons would be primitively designed (maybe even comprised of common tools), and their hand-to-hand combat tactics would probably focus on the weaknesses in their enemy's armor. However, for the purposes of creating such a martial art, the U.S. military finds itself on the opposite end of the spectrum. It has advanced weaponry, armor, and maneuverability; using tactics and techniques from the latter group would be more appropriate.

I eventually learned, while composing the curriculum for my women's self-protection class, that there isn't a generic technique system that encompasses all aspects of combat. Women's self-defense is different from tournament karate, which is different from kickboxing, which is different from judo, etc. Thus, when creating any military system, one has to create it based on the real needs of that military, needs that address soldiers in a variety of situations: at an embassy, soldiers at a detainee facility, soldiers on the battlefield, etc. One might find that they may create small technique systems for each one of these needs. The point here is that, in the honest creation of any combative system, one has to sit and ponder an enemy's strengths, weaknesses, mindset, and tactics, as well as their own.

Unlike techniques and needs, I have found that principles and concepts seem to transcend time. For instance, the principles for throwing an opponent, with or without armor, say that it is best to keep a low center of gravity and get the opponent off-balance. Another principle says that if you push something and it doesn't move, you will probably push with more force the second time. A third principle states that the taller you stand, the more off-balance you are. Principles don't lose their validity. However, with tactics and techniques this is not always the case. Think about the battle lines employed in the Civil War, where soldiers would form into long lines, two ranks deep, across from their enemy. In the 19th century, battle lines were the primary way of delivering the most firepower. However, as technology advanced with the development of long-range rifles, cannons, etc., this tactic became obsolete, even suicidal. Thus, using principles as a base of creation is more feasible and longer lasting than using tactics and techniques.

Continued Evolution

When I began the refinement of the B.P.C. curriculum's combative techniques, combative needs and beliefs were the topic of discussion at my chow hall table every day in Iraq. This was a great opportunity to ask questions, because in the chow hall (dining facility) you could easily find yourself sitting across from the upper echelon of military leadership. It was in this setting that I was able to evolve this new system to a new level. It was the equivalent of what I believed was done throughout history. As a soldier, I had a very narrow perspective of the sprawling military; talking to and working with several others is the key to gaining greater perspective. It is evident that many systems don't do this. My teacher once told me that it isn't wise to assume that one man alone can think of all the answers, for one man will never be as wise as ten. Consider the creation and evolution of the automobile or airplane, for example. No one single person was behind the evolution of these vehicles. Before and after their inception, an array of people added to the creation and development of these machines.

Instead of following the logic of talking, learning, and evolving, all too often the situation has been one individual who was in the military (or who sees the profitability of the military as a client), who takes his martial art and says: "I believe this will work for a service member." Although some of his choices may be wise, he can definitely miss a few things. That is why it is important to actively seek input from others. Pride sometimes stops this from happening. (The same can be said of ignorance and, in the worst cases, greed.)

The battlefield is a collection of living things, and it changes like a living thing. As equipment becomes better, tactics change and enemies become more focused, so must the service members and their combatives must make adjustments. B.P.C. is dedicated to evolution and change. It is based on the full range of operational experiences. Thus, the plainclothes embassy soldier is taken into account, as well as the M.P. in garrison, and the infantryman in Iraq or Afghanistan. However, the battlefield armor-clad soldier is its primary focus, because this area has, for so long, been overlooked or not properly addressed by other combative systems.

chapter 5
THE BASICS

BASIC STANCE

There are three stances in the B.P.C. curriculum. However, the focus is on the first basic stance in the Basic and Intermediate Individual Training modules. This stance closely resembles that of the classic pistol Isosceles stance. The soldier stands square, with knees bent, feet shoulder width apart, back slightly bent forward, weapon in the right hand, extended and hovering in front of the solar plexus, and the left hand hovering close to the body behind the right.

The placement of the hands is important, because they offer an inanimate primary barrier (weapon) and an alternative barrier (rear hand) between the service member's vital torso and his opponent. The centering of the hands also allows for almost equal travel distance from the center of the body to any of the upper regions of the body.

Placing the weapon up front like this has both advantages and disadvantages. In the other modules of B.P.C. training, there are other placements for the weapon, but this is the basic position.

Another reason this stance was chosen is because it is familiar to service members, who usually adopt and use this stance, or a modified version of it, when learning assault and shooting tactics.

Because B.P.C. is designed for service members on the battlefield, it strongly focuses on wearing full combative gear, which is designed to give maximum protection to the service member's torso. By facing the opponent in this way, service members create multiple barriers of defense, thus increasing his or her level of protection.

Balance, Stability, Efficient Motion, and Non-commitment

The B.P.C. basic stance was also chosen because it allows for maximum balance, stability, efficiency of movement, and non-commitment. Strip away the combat gear, put on a basketball uniform and you have a defensive basketball stance; throw on a football uniform and you have a defensive back's stance; grab a tennis racket and you have a tennis stance. The B.P.C. basic stance is

not a B.P.C. original; it is a universal stance that allows for the most effective and efficient means of movement in any direction.

Balance

Bent knees and spreading the feet at a shoulder's width allows for a low center of gravity and a stable base, which is needed for balance, quick reaction, and smooth movement. Whether we realize it or not, we bend our knees every time we step. This is done to gain stability while the body transitions from two legs to one in a normal step. We have learned over time (changing from the straight-legged walk of an infant to the natural walk of an adult) that the straighter our legs are, the more off-balance we will be. This can definitely be seen when walking on a slippery surface, such as snow, ice, or mud. If you were to watch a person trying to walk upright on these slippery surfaces, you will immediately witness the difficulty they would have with their balance.

If that person were to fall and stand back up, you would see them lower their stance to help gain stability. If you watch a log rolling competition, for instance, you'll see how deep the competitors' knees are bent in order to maintain their balance. Consciously and subconsciously, we know that a lower center of gravity and wider base means greater stability.

Another situation that can contribute to a loss of balance is when a person is carrying a heavy load. It becomes more difficult to maintain stability if the legs aren't bent, the feet aren't separated for a wider base, and the back isn't upright with a slight bend. The higher a person is and the closer together their feet are, the more precarious will be their balance. The way we usually compensate for this is by bending our knees more and straightening our back. Even as a child playing with dominoes, or building blocks, you learned that a wider and taller base essentially changed the center of gravity, giving you more stability at a greater height. The same principle applies here. However, instead of being able to build ourselves upward, we can place more weight on our bodies, such as wearing an I.B.A. with a full combat load. To correct this, one has to lower his or her center of gravity and widen his or her base, allowing for greater stability.

In addition to the lower center of gravity and the wider base, keeping the back upright, but with a slight forward angle, will also improve balance. When weight is added to the torso, moving at the waist alone puts unnatural strain on the lower back, which could cause injuries. Also, exaggerated leaning in any direction with the torso will lead to a loss in equilibrium. Leaning too far in any direction with this added weight creates a commitment to that direction. For this reason, leaning makes it less efficient and more difficult to move in any direction other than that which the person is already leaning.

The center of neutral balance is that point in your positioning that provides perfect balance and also allows for quick movement in any given direction. Leaning breaks this center of neutral balance, while leaning too far forward could cause you to fall forward. To change direction when leaning, you have to move back to a neutral balance and then change direction, thus adding to the time it takes to perform a movement.

Quick Reaction Time

I'll now review the reason why this basic stance allows for quicker reaction time. One aspect of reaction time is the time it takes for your mind to perceive a situation using your eyes, process it, and create a response. Another aspect of reaction time is the execution of that response. I am sure you agree that the less your body has to transition in order to execute this response, the quicker and more efficient your reaction will be.

Imagine three people having a race. The first person is positioned two steps away from the finish line, with the second person four steps away, and the final person six steps away. It is obvious that the person who only takes two steps would reach the line first. Whether it is taking fewer steps or making fewer movements, less is better. The lesson here is that if one needs to move, they have to sink their knees to be efficient and increase reaction time. Starting with the knees bent means fewer movements and quicker reaction time.

Anyone who knows even a little about professional football has heard of Barry Sanders, a former star running back for the Detroit Lions. Barry made a name for himself by having an uncanny ability to confuse and avoid opposing defenders through a series of phenomenally quick changes in direction and speed. Although I am not an avid football fan, the first time I saw Barry run, I had to see more of him. I would watch and record his games religiously, trying to figure out what made his movements so phenomenal and different. I played his highlights repeatedly and in slow-motion. One thing I eventually realized was that, besides having incredibly strong legs, Barry's real secret was in his low center of gravity. Barry stood 5'6," which made him much shorter than his opponents. In addition to being short, he also crouched very low while running. The combination of the two created the perfect body dynamic for quick reaction time. When he needed to change direction, he was in the perfect form to do it without making major adjustments.

Smooth Movement

During my executive protection training in civilian life and my Military Operation in Urban Terrain (M.O.U.T.) training in the military, I noticed something universal about movement with weapons. No matter what weapons stance you adopt, the key to smooth movement with your weapon at the ready, or while firing, was having bent knees. Bending one's knees while stepping alleviates the bobbing, and in some cases rocking, motions that take place when one walks. As I touched on previously, when a person takes a step, they go from a straight-leg position to a bent-knee position. With each step, a person transitions from straight legs to bent legs repetitively, creating a bobbing motion. By sinking the knees and consciously keeping the body from returning to an erect position, one keeps this bobbing to a minimum, providing smoother movement and greatly enhancing shooting accuracy. Besides stability and quicker reaction in full body movement, the smoothness at which one is able to move his body adds to his efficiency.

Understanding these concepts led to the use of the bent-knee stances in multiple sports. This is also why this stance was chosen as the B.P.C. basic stance. The B.P.C. basic stance isn't impervious to vulnerability; no stance is. This stance has weaknesses, just like any other. However, thanks to its similarity to a firing stance, and its noncommittal and stable quality, this stance proves itself to be highly effective and efficient.

Noncommittal

The B.P.C. basic stance requires that an equal amount of the body's weight be distributed on both legs. This equal distribution allows for one to move in all directions with an equal amount of efficiency. This also allows for a service member to strike equally effectively from each region of the body. In the uncertainty of combat, it is very effective when one attacks or defends from this stance.

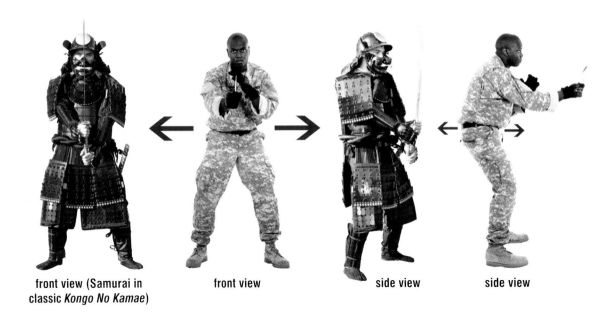

front view (Samurai in classic *Kongo No Kamae*)   front view   side view   side view

Basic Defenses

There are three major types of defensive measures used in the B.P.C., one of which is conditional. The first and most important is movement of the body, the second is using external weapons or limbs as defensive tools, and the third is conditionally based on a service member's use of body armor.

Primary Defense: Full Body Movement

Similar to boxing or other combat arts, movement is very important. In boxing, where one of the main objectives is to knock an opponent unconscious with a series of blows to the head, it is imperative that a boxer learns how to keep his head in continual transition (bobbing and weaving). This makes one's head a harder target for an opponent to strike. This movement also helps save energy, because absorbing a strike diminishes energy.

So, like the boxer, the B.P.C. practitioner is taught that movement is a primary defense. However, the movement in B.P.C. is very different than in boxing because there are no set parameters or arena. Because service members could find themselves in an array of different environments, wearing different equipment, it is imperative that movement is basic and efficient. Also, because service members can't spend years training in B.P.C., it is essential to use movements that are simple and easy to remember. For this reason, at the basic level, B.P.C. focuses on three major full-body movements. These movements are the slide back (a small hop, keeping close to the ground), the 45-degree slide step (a step that is more like a slide, because it is so close to the ground), and the open door movement (a movement that mimics a hinged door opening). These movements are executed with the entire body moving as a single unit. This movement is done to ensure that the entire body is out of harm's way and to help maintain balance. B.P.C. practitioners in the basic phase learn to move the same way with or without armor, therefore decreasing the learning time and increasing efficiency and effectiveness.

One problem with some military fighting systems is a primary focus on defending with weapons of advantage, weapons of opportunity, and personal weapons. I believe this is a mistake, because when an assailant attacks, he or she views something on your body as a target. In a perfect world, it is simple to say that I will take my arm or leg and block what is coming at me.

However, in a not-so-perfect world, a realist understands that a number of factors can render this type of block ineffective. Perhaps your assailant is too strong or has so much momentum behind their attack that their arm, stick, or knife forces its way past your block.

Another possibility is that you believe the attack is coming from the wrong angle and when you try to block, you miss (e.g. boxers are usually taught not to reach out to block because it exposes them and it is hard to effectively connect their block with an opponent's strike).

Figure 1

Figure 2

Both of these scenarios point to the frightening fact that the body, the original target, is to some degree still in the same position as when the assailant began his or her attack. Therefore, if this initial block doesn't succeed, the target will most likely be struck. For this reason, B.P.C. focuses on moving the body, or target, out of the way as the primary defense, and using the external weapons or limb blocks in conjunction as an alternate defense or backup. This also makes for quicker and more efficient counterstrikes.

In (Figure 1), the attacker (right) is stabbing down at the defender's chest. In (Figure 2), the defender moves off-line, placing his body out of harm's way,

Figure 2b

while in (Figure 4) using his weapon to secure and counterattack the attacker's striking arm.

Figure 4

Figure 4b

Alternate Defense: External Weapons or Limbs

External weapons refer to weapons of advantage, weapons of opportunity, and personal weapons, which were discussed earlier. These weapons make up the alternate defense method for B.P.C. As mentioned, many martial arts systems use these as their primary defense. Far too often, you see a combat instructor teaching someone to hold his or her ground and block the attack, but if you miss or are overwhelmed by the opponent's strength or force, you will get struck.

In B.P.C., using the limb or weapon to defend against an attack happens in conjunction with body movement. This gives the practitioner the assurance that his or her body is safe from the initial attack, even if he or she doesn't block or counterstrike effectively.

Contingency Defense: I.B.A.

For service members in I.B.A., there is a contingency defense in the event that both the primary and the alternate defenses fail. This contingency is simply not placing soft, unprotected limbs between your opponent and your body armor. If a person attacks you with a blunt trauma weapon and you were unsuccessful at stopping it, positioning yourself so that the body armor takes the blunt of the force is preferred. One misconception that is closely examined and discussed in B.P.C. is the advisability of using this tactic when a knife is involved. Many people believe the myth that Kevlar is stab proof. Well, unless there is new technology I don't know about, the truth is that Kevlar is not stab proof at all.

When bullets strike a target they flatten out from the impact. Kevlar is designed to distribute that impact throughout the vest, dissipating outward the forward force that typically pushes the bullet through the body. With a thrusting knife, the driving force is constant because someone is holding the knife. Also, unlike a bullet, a knife doesn't flatten out, and all the force is focused at the point, allowing for greater overall pressure in one spot. This is what allows a knife to pass through Kevlar. Consequently, the stab vest was introduced in correctional facilities to protect correctional officers from sustaining severe stab wounds from inmates. Today, there are vests that are both stab and bulletproof, but the military doesn't have them. In addition

to not flattening out like a bullet, knives can change trajectory in the hands of its wielder and therefore could penetrate places on the body where there is no armor.

However, there are two situations in which Kevlar, in particular I.B.A., can protect you from knife wounds. First, if an assailant stabbed you in the strike plate of a vest or magazine, and, second, if the assailant attacked with a slicing motion instead of a stabbing motion.

Not much explanation is needed for why, in these situations, one would be protected. Just to clarify, the advantage of the I.B.A. is as the third alternative if all else fails. If, in an imperfect world, one can defend with the first two options, then so be it.

Basic Weaponry

We have all heard the saying that the mind is the greatest weapon one possesses. I partially agree. I say that the mind is the greatest instrument we possess. However, the mind alone does not defend against nor can it cause physical harm; the body does. In the traditional sense of the word, the mind is not a weapon, but one's body is the first physical tool that can cause physical harm. The body is recognized as the first weapon in B.P.C., but there are also two others: weapons of advantage and weapons of opportunity.

Personal Weapons

Personal weapons are body parts that can be used as offensive or defensive weapons. B.P.C. teaches service members how to use hands, head, elbows, forearms, knees, feet, shoulders, and shins. By learning the use of various personal weapons, a service member becomes more effective and efficient in combat by increasing the number of striking positions. Traditionally, many military systems focus on using only the hands, feet, shins, and elbows, limiting the versatility of a combatant.

Weapons of Advantage

Weapons of advantage are viewed in B.P.C. as weapons that the soldier would normally carry as a part of his or her combat or non-combat equipment. These weapons include rifles, pistols, knives, extendable batons, pepper spray, etc. It is obvious how a rifle or pistol could be a weapon of advantage in their primary functions, but, as discussed earlier, even if they are no longer serviceable as a projectile weapon, they could still be used skillfully as a blunt trauma or bludgeon weapon.

Weapons of Opportunity

Weapons of opportunity are objects in one's surrounding that can be used as offensive or defensive weapons—a hammer, stick, bottle, chain, brick, etc. B.P.C. teaches the service member how to use a multitude of weapons of opportunity. This way, the service member does not have to rely on pure primal instinct because he or she does not effectively know how to use an object as a weapon.

Instilling in a soldier the knowledge of multiple weapons gives a greater sense of confidence and security in knowing that he or she is never without a means of defense.

Angles & Levels

The Nine Angles

In my B.P.C. classes, I am repeatedly asked why it is important to know these nine angles. When I first started teaching, it surprised me that people would ask this, especially people who have trained in some other martial art or combat system. However, from my own experience with learning and teaching, I eventually realized that the simple things are sometimes the most overlooked.

The reason I make these nine angles a focal point of the B.P.C. curriculum is because the majority of attacks will come from one of these nine angles. Training in a way that forces the practitioner to internalize these angles is important. The nine-angle drills practiced in B.P.C. allows for a structured way to perform and discern these angles. The drills teach a practitioner that whether it is a boxer throwing a right hook, a kickboxer throwing a front kick, a tae kwon do expert delivering an axe kick, or a grappler shooting in for a tackle, the attacks will likely travel along one of these angles. Understanding this concept narrows a practitioner's scope of the attacks possible by an opponent. From this narrowing of a vast array of potential attacks, a practitioner is better able to understand the relationship between a kick approaching the left side of the head and a punch following that same line/angle. Comprehending this simplifies combat training, teaching, and dynamics. Grasping this allows a practitioner to see that a kick and a punch following the same line of attack are not different entities to be dealt with using separate techniques.

The nine basic angles of attack are just that—basic. They are nine general directions from which an assailant—skilled or unskilled—is likely to attack. I wish I were old enough or cool enough to take credit for discovering these angles myself, but, sorry, I don't win the prize for the most original combative instructor this year or any other year. The truth is, like most combative systems today, the concepts of the nine angles can be found in many different martial arts (some arts teach more than nine angles of attack). Practitioners going to these schools spend years mastering how to defend and strike from these angles.

The Three Levels

Teaching the angles of attack alone is not complete without teaching the three levels of attack. Both are needed to complete the proper skills of avoidance, interception, and attack for B.P.C. The three levels of attack basically divide the body into three regions: the high level, the mid level, and the lower level.

High Level

The high level encompasses the head and neck regions of the body. This level, as you can imagine, is one of the most vital regions of the body. The head is instinctively the most likely target of any attacker trying to incapacitate his opponent.

Mid Level

The mid level encompasses the torso and the arms. This region of the body is important because it houses some of the most vital organs for any human's survival. This is proven by the fact that when one is under extreme duress, the mind and body pull most of the blood from the extremities to the torso for protection, use, and functionality. This is also why today's body armor is designed primarily to protect the torso.

Lower Level

The lower level encompasses the genitals and the legs. Although this is not normally the most common area to be attacked, this is without a doubt an important level, for reasons of mobility (as well as other important reasons).

The combination of the nine angles and the three levels gives a practitioner a simple but effective understanding of attacks and attack movements during hand-to-hand combat. This combination provides a comprehensive and easy to follow method of internalizing a defensive and attacking vision that is required in close-quarters hand-to-hand combat.

chapter 6

UNDERSTANDING DISTANCE

*Anyone can throw a punch, swing a stick, or rush in and wrestle someone
to the ground. However, understanding how to control space and controlling the space between you and the attacker is much more difficult.*

Controlling Distance

No matter what the cause, once a battle starts it becomes a struggle to control
space. One commander moves his troops to fight and gain control of space;
the other commander uses his troops to defend that space.

In the realm of the single combatant, B.P.C focuses on three primary zones
of attack and defense that represent position in relationship to one's opponent
in distance, or what I call "space." These zones are called the outer, mid, and
inner proximities. These zones are not specific to B.P.C. Variations of these
zones are present in many other combat systems, as well as in military tactics.

Outer Proximity

The outer zone is a neutral distance between two opponents, in which they
are not able to inflict harm on each other without the use of an overtly aggressive movement, a projectile, or a projectile weapon. The outer zone is a
strong focus of the B.P.C. curriculum because it is in this zone that one, consciously or unconsciously, sizes up an opponent. Unless projectile weapons are
involved, this is the safest zone from which to discern an opponent's intention.
As stated, if a person's intentions are hostile, he or she has to move closer

to the defender's position, which could provide the defender with a possible advantage. To practice familiarity with this zone, B.P.C. practitioners usually face each other and extend their right arms and hands in front of their bodies until only their fingertips touch.

Mid Proximity

The mid zone is a zone that is pretty common to Americans, for it is the zone that many of us subconsciously use when we talk to one another. Although it

is comfortable to talk from this position for Americans, it is stressed to soldiers on the frontlines that one should avoid being in this zone while dealing with those whose intentions are not clear. This zone is the easiest zone from which a hostile can strike. However, while engaging offensively or defensively, this zone is the primary—and in some cases preferred—zone. To practice familiarity with this zone, B.P.C. practitioners usually face each other and extend their right arms. Because the fist is one of the primary personal weapons used in this zone, participants reach to their opponent's shoulders, arms outstretched. Besides punches, a variety of kicks and close grappling are also used in this zone.

Inner Proximity

This zone is arguably the most dangerous. It is sometimes referred to as the clinch or grapple zone, because of the instinctive desire and ability to grab someone within this proximity. Americans usually have a problem being comfortable in this position, because this proximity breaks our personal space boundaries. This zone is usually not culturally acceptable when dealing with unfamiliar individuals. When I was in Iraq, my comrades and I found it very unsettling when local nationals would come very close, entering our inner proximity to talk to us. I believe one of the things that makes this proximity so dangerous is the short amount of distance that it would take for someone's hand to travel to one of your weapons or to grab you. Some of the primary personal weapons used in this proximity are knees, forearms, elbows, shoulders, and head-butts. The fist can be used in an uppercut fashion. However, the elbow is usually preferred over the fist because of leverage and positioning. To practice familiarity with this zone, B.P.C. practitioners usually face each other and extend their right arms. They then move close enough to each other so that the inner bend at the elbow is beside their training partner's head.

Studying and understanding these proximities helps a service member grasp the concept of distancing and the levels of potential danger that comes with each proximity.

chapter 7

WINNING CONCEPTS

Sometimes going through a river is more hazardous
and less efficient than finding a way around it.

I remember once asking a Ranger at Fort Benning what he thought the difference was between how Rangers and Special Forces soldiers handle missions. His reply was: "If a group of Rangers come to a wall, they will beat on the wall until they break through it. However, if a group of Special Forces soldiers come to a wall, they will find their way over, under, or around it."

This description reminded me of the difference between the fire and water elements in the Japanese martial art that I study. Fire represents the thoughts and tactics that are hard-charging, straight forward, and overwhelming. Much like a fire in a forest, it consumes everything in sight and the more you beat at it, adding oxygen, the more it is fueled and continues to grow. On the other hand, water represents thoughts and tactics that are scientific and flowing. Water, like waves in the ocean moving back and forth to shore, moves one to a position where he or she can discern (or create) a weakness in his opponent and exploit it with a full assault.

From the Ranger's description, I saw how Rangers think and fight like fire: in a hard-charging, straight forward and overwhelming way; their brothers-in-arms, Special Forces, has a more analytical, scientific, and watery approach to combat.

Obviously, there is a place for both of these combat units in the U.S. Army, and both serve their purposes very well. Yet, when it comes to combatives,

I believe that there is usually only a focus on the fire aspect of combat. Many of the systems I have seen are mostly comprised of techniques where a service member rushes in on an attacker in an attempt to overwhelm him or her.

This seems to be the favored view among many systems. While this mentality teaches the service member aggression and fosters a fighting spirit, it can also be very hazardous. One instance where this might be dangerous is when dealing with improvised explosive devices (I.E.D.s). Insurgents often use secondary I.E.D.s to wound or kill quick response forces who rush in to help and recover those wounded by the initial I.E.D. A more watery approach of properly assessing the area around an I.E.D detonation becomes paramount before rushing to help those in need. Also, with the fire attitude of combat, one can find oneself in a tough situation when the opponent is stronger or bigger or when the defender can't intercept the initial attack fast enough to render it useless; meeting force with force only works some of the time.

I'm not saying I believe there is a perfect system. I am saying that any system's focus should be geared toward giving the user more than the tools of strength and speed. There are many situations where the fire mentality works well, such as when doing a cordon and search, or a direct action mission. When entering a house by force, it is good to keep moving and clearing rooms as fast and as safely as possible, giving a potential enemy as little time as possible to take counteraction.

However, imagine a scenario where you are on a direct action mission. You enter a room expecting to destroy any living person you see. Quickly scanning left, you fix your sights on a person with a knife in his hand. Instinctively, you squeeze the trigger but nothing happens. No matter how well trained you may be, you will probably be lying to yourself if you think you would not hesitate for a second. You might, and you might not. However, one thing is pretty clear: You just tried to take this person's life and he or she knows it. If he or she hasn't surrendered or your partner hasn't shot him or her, he or she is likely going to try to attack you before you reload your weapon. Rushing in to attack him might be your instinctive answer. But if it isn't, have you undergone training that prepared you for both reactions?

Some might say that this is not a realistic situation. When I went to war, though, I quickly learned that anything is possible.

Just as an example, every Monday I cleaned my pistol magazines in fear that they would stick due to sand and grit. Well, one Wednesday I came back from a mission, took my magazine out of my weapon, and my bullets just fell out of the magazine. The springs in the magazine had gone bad; when I went to get new ones I found that this happens often. My point is that in war anything could happen.

Systems that hold true to a service member's operational realism should (like the Rangers and Special Forces communities), encompass both fire and water strategies to combatives. Therefore, when an opponent is stronger or faster, the practitioner can still take advantage of an opponent. This is like the Army: When a wall needs to be destroyed they send a Ranger, and when it needs to be circumvented or in some way manipulated they send Special Forces.

If you want to see the fire mentality in action for yourself, go to an amateur boxing event. I remember going to a contest like this for service members, much like the Toughman competition in which anyone (men or women) could join, and were paired by weight class. Most of the fighters were pure fire in the way they fought. The bell would ring and the combatants would run straight at each other and start swinging for the fences. Usually the winner was the fighter who knocked his opponent out with a lucky shot or who landed the most blows. You could tell who had some training and who didn't, but overall it was an all-out slugfest.

The most memorable fights featured a small, older man that everyone thought was in for a serious beating, not just because he was visibly older than all the other fighters but also because for all three of his fights he seemed to get stuck with the younger fighters with better physiques. Each time he fought, his strategy became more visible. He would put his guard up and move around as the younger fighter came in, swinging and chasing him. The older fighter

took a lot of hits in the first round, but for the last two rounds guess who was dousing the fire with water?

This older fighter, who came to be called "Old Man," would open up a can of butt-kicking on his exhausted opponent, using a conservative amount of well-placed punches. Each fight ended with him as the winner and his younger, well-built opponent as the loser.

This was a perfect example of how using the water mindset allows your opponent to create his or her own weakness so you can exploit it. It would be different if you were always stronger and faster, or always knew how and when you would have to use your skill, but this is not the case in every situation.

During the battlefield ground combat (B.G.C.) portion of my B.P.C. class in Ramadi, we came to the point where the practitioners were competent enough to start drilling the techniques in Set One. They started the drill on their knees, the assailant had a knife and the defender was unarmed.

At my cue, the assailant would attack. The defender's task was to grab the attacker's wrists or forearms, and then try to maneuver the attacker into a position from which the defender could successfully utilize one of the B.G.C. techniques. The attacker also had a job, which was to help by trying to maneuver his victim to a position in which the supposed victim could pull off one of the techniques. Some reading this might say that sounds simple. However, when I said, "Start," the training went out the window and immediately, no matter who had a weight or strength advantage, it devolved into a wrestling stalemate.

The first thing that came to the practitioners' minds was to shoot in and wrestle, whether they had the advantage or not—the typical "beat the wall until it falls" fire mentality. It was evident that the fire mentality was the overall mindset. However, as both attacker and defender were working in the same element, mainly what occurred was a struggle that wasted energy and got neither person anywhere.

When it was time for reflection, critiquing, and the after action report, it was difficult for the practitioners to grasp the concept that, because they were working with a certain number of tools (techniques), they had to find or create a situation in which they would be able to use those tools. Even if I had years to teach them every technique in the book, they would still only use five of the most comfortable techniques. Unfortunately, their opponents wouldn't always attack in a way that would enable the practitioner to use those five techniques. Sometimes the practitioner would have to find or create a situation that would enable them to take advantage of one of these techniques. This type of thinking is "water thinking," whereas "fire thinking" involves being so connected with an attacker that you overwhelm him or her before he or she gains momentum (i.e., someone starts to throw a punch and, just as they pull it back, you move in and strike first).

To help explain this in greater depth, I told the practitioners that when I studied grappling, my instructor would have me practice two or three moves for hours. Then, I would have to grapple someone and try to use only those moves. This was difficult because my opponent would be trying to get me into a position for submission. Thus, it was difficult to force my opponent into a position where I could use one of the practiced moves. Eventually, I learned that I could create such situations by making my opponent think that I was making a mistake, or allowing him or her to feel like he or she was dominating—a water approach. I learned that I could control aggressive people through the illusion of passiveness and control passive or less-aggressive people by being aggressive. This "taking on the form of opposition" helped me mitigate sense-less struggle, conserve energy, and accomplish my goals.

Although the primary focus of this drill was to teach the defending service member how to transition between elements and control his adversary, the sec-ondary function was to teach the service member playing the assailant how to control his energy. For the practitioner playing the assailant, it was impor-tant to control the energy that he was expending. This training helped him understand the flow of energy in combat. Thus, if he can control his energy and positioning, consciously and subconsciously, it will make it harder for an opponent to take advantage of him when he is in a real combative situation.

To recap: rushing at a problem won't necessarily be the solution. Sometimes one is not in a position to respond quickly or can't discern what is happening fast enough. For this reason, B.P.C. teaches a mixture of fire and water tech-niques, giving the soldier a wider range of choices during life threatening situations.

chapter 8

EXHAUSTIVE MEASURES

It is 10 a.m. at Camp Ramadi in Iraq. As I look around the training room in the Moral, Welfare & Recreation fitness center, I see faces that radiate exhaustion and fatigue. Dripping sweat from underneath their I.B.A., my fellow comrades and B.P.C. training partners stand ready to perform their next killing technique. Just by looking in their eyes you can see that, although drained, they are not lacking the ability or confidence needed to successfully engage and defeat the next opponent, and, if needed, also defeat another. For as long as the opponents keep coming, they will keep neutralizing the threat with necessary force.

The military loves its PT and whenever there is an opportunity for PT the opportunity is taken. Combatives are no different; the military usually steers towards systems that incorporate exercises into its curriculum. I totally understand this mindset, and I definitely believe that it has its place.

When I was creating the B.P.C. curriculum, I had to wonder, with the short amount of time I would have to make service members efficient and effective, how much time did I want to spend on exercises or calisthenics? My final answer was: not much time, if any. There are four main schools of thought on this topic: the first is that anyone about to take part in any combative activity needs to warm up and stretch before the activity; the second is that because the ultimate goal is to get participants to a level in which they don't have to use strength to achieve success when executing the techniques, exhausting them with exercises before making them practice the techniques will keep them from using muscle; the third is that such exercises are necessary to improve the service member's overall stamina and conditioning: finally, some see the exercise as a form of indoctrination or confidence building. Making someone push past the limits of exhaustion and then successfully execute a technique shows them that they always have a little more, and proves to them that the technique works.

Before I joined the Army, I lived in Ohio. While there, in addition to attending my main martial arts school, I would also train with an Ultimate Fighting Championship (UFC) trainer and MMA fighter who was helping train a soon-to-be Middleweight UFC champion. I wanted to work on my ground-fighting skills and needed new training partners, and I was told that this was the place to be. My first two times there I trained in the Brazilian Jiu-Jitsu class first, and then I would take the round robin free-grappling class. Something that I noticed about the Brazilian Jiu-Jitsu portion of training was that we only worked on three techniques over the course of a two-hour class. By the end of class I was exhausted. Just when I thought it was over, it was time to "roll" (free response grapple), with the purpose of trying to successfully execute one of the three techniques we learned earlier. The class was grueling. When it was over, really over, I barely had enough energy to make it home.

During my training, two amazing things happened. The first was that I was able to successfully use one of the techniques; it was a great feeling of accomplishment that instilled confidence. The other was learning that the reason I was able to execute the technique was because of the two-hour practice sessions, which helped my body and mind remember the movements.

This was not the first time that I had experienced this feeling at a school, but it is a perfect example of what brought me to my training philosophy in B.P.C.

In ancient Japan, many schools focused on repetition of techniques to build strength, confidence, focus, efficiency, and effectiveness. In this same spirit, the

B.P.C. philosophy is exhaustion through training and repetition, not exhaustion through unconnected exercises and calisthenics. It is no secret that repetition is the key to mastering anything. So why waste precious time on anything else, especially if energized training will have the same effect?

If you still don't understand my reason for this philosophy, think about it like this: there is usually only a short amount of time allotted for combatives training in the military. Classes, usually a few hours a day, can range from one week to a few weeks. However, anyone who knows anything about martial arts training understands the difficulty of trying to train someone to be proficient in a martial art in just a few weeks. Therefore, using every bit of time for training is paramount. A second reason I chose this philosophy is because, as a soldier, I know maintaining physical fitness standards are a part of military life; unit PT is usually conducted every day. It is safe to assume that most military personnel are, to some degree, physically fit. It is not the job of B.P.C. (or other combative systems) to make service members PT studs; the service does a great job of that. It is B.P.C.'s job to train service members on how to be efficient and effective combatants. The B.P.C. curriculum doesn't incorporate log runs, buddy carries, bear crawls, duck walks, Iron Mikes, etc. However, there are tons of knife drills, stick drills, fall drills, grapple drills, etc. This ensures muscle fatigue and then focuses remaining strength on efficient and effective execution.

Through fatigue, the brain is able to subconsciously remember a technique's movements; through repetition, the conscious mind commits the technique to memory. Service members leave class exhausted, but from constant execution of techniques not on pointless strengthening exercises. If you had a limited time to learn something that could save your life, wouldn't you want to spend as much time as possible learning that thing?

Another aspect of the B.P.C. curriculum that I carefully reviewed was stretching and warm-ups. This was not just a matter of time constraints, like the repetition of techniques, it was also a question of safety. Mission readiness is important to military service members. Service members have to live with a certain level of risk every day, whether deployed or in garrison. I know this all too well, being a part of the Special Ops community. However, the goal of every First Sergeant and Commander (or other service equivalent) is to not lose subordinates due to training accidents. Unfortunately, service members often get hurt during training events, and combatives is no different. B.P.C.'s goal is to train soldiers as safely as possible while maintaining the standard of producing efficient and effective warfighters. In following this standard, I debated with myself as to how much, if any, stretching should be done before and after class. The question that spawned the answer was: "If a soldier was in the field, how much time would he or she have to stretch before getting into an altercation?" The answer is, unless the conflict is staged, none. Therefore, I've elected to incorporate a minimal amount of stretching before class.

This choice was also guided by the contents of the technique's curriculum. How many of the techniques required flexibility, and how many would put unnatural strain on the practitioner? The answers were "not many" and "none," therefore stretching is not a main focus of training. Thus, only a few minutes are used for stretching. Warm-ups, on the other hand, are important. In keeping with the philosophy described in the beginning paragraph on this chapter, warm-ups are done with drills that are incorporated in the techniques. In this manner, no actual training time is lost.

chapter 9

BATTLEFIELD GROUND COMBAT

Ground fighting for soldiers! For proving yourself in the ring maybe, but on the urban battlefield never! On the unforgiving battlefield, where life depends on shooting, moving, and communicating, grappling has no place (unless you are trying to get to your feet after being knocked down). On the battlefield there is rough and rugged terrain, razor wire, short lines of sight, rubble, etc., none of which match the smooth and controlled environment of a gym or ring. On the battlefield, the ground is the worst place to find yourself, because it is hard to follow the "shoot, move, communicate" principles of warfare as well as support your team.

GROUND FIGHTING AND THE MISSION

Grappling and ground fighting arts experienced a "boom" in the 1990s. Since then, it seems that everywhere you go someone is teaching grappling. This can be easily accredited to the rise in fame of grappling in the competitive arena. Even in the military, it seems as though "combatives" has become synonymous with "ground fighting." If you need convincing, go to any of the popular search engines and type in "Military Combatives," you will get links for a myriad of sites that show ground fighting.

This is understandable due to the competitive spirit that ground fighting can build in a person. There is something about grappling, trying to get someone into a position where they submit, that is very primal. A second reason for grappling's popularity is that many people believe that most fights end up on the ground. I personally, along with three study groups, did a survey on how often fights go to the ground, and the results might burst a few bubbles. What we found after surveying over one hundred street fights, was that at some point someone in the fight, if not both individuals, fell, or were knocked or thrown to the ground. However, their natural inclination was not to stay there and grapple but to get back to their feet. In very few of these cases did one or both

individuals stay on the ground for more than 2-4 seconds. In the rare instance during a fight where someone spent extended time on the ground he or she was being held there and hit by their standing opponent.

The study group discussed many theories on why this might be, but one of the best theories was that it might be a part of our primal instinct. Much like animals in nature fighting; the objective is to get bigger and higher than your opponent. This creates a sense of dominance in the conflict and can subconsciously create a feeling of submission in the opponent. Military personnel can understand this concept by thinking of the dynamic between a private and a drill sergeant during basic training. If you would like to explore more about this survey you can go to my website at **www.bpccombatives.com**.

Furthermore, many groundfighting enthusiasts claim that ground fighting is the most efficient way to finish off an opponent in a close-quarters hand-to-hand combat encounter. This statement is pretty broad, so the question that comes to my mind first is: What is the situation that a person using this statement might be talking about? If this person is talking about trying to subdue an unruly local national in an embassy, a detained individual, an adversary in an arena, or a buddy in a sand-filled pit, they may be correct. But on the battlefield, where armor and weapons are involved, I beg to differ.

Before making broad statements like this, certain aspects of the different missions and combat scenarios need to be viewed.

Let me review, very quickly, the primary mission statements of two Army special operations groups:

> *"The Rangers' primary mission is to engage the enemy in close-combat and direct-fire battles. This mission includes direct-action operations, raids, personnel and special equipment recovery, in addition to conventional or special light-infantry operations."*

"U.S. Special Forces missions include direct action operations, unconventional warfare, special recon, and counterterrorism."

Judging by the description of their primary missions, there are only a few situations where these groups will be on the battlefield without body armor or multiple weapons. I think the most efficient way to subdue an enemy in close-quarters hand-to-hand combat would be the use of an available weapon. As I stated earlier, there are scenarios where one will not be authorized to use deadly force, but on the battlefield (for which I primarily created B.P.C.) one must use whatever force is necessary to save one's life. I believe that many of the people who make the aforementioned claims, or teach primarily ground fighting for military combatives, aren't properly applying its use. I am not saying they aren't great ground fighters; they just haven't properly assessed the operational realism of today's service member.

The next aspect that I review is the use of the word "efficiency," and how it relates to natural body movement and positioning. I hear so much about ground fighting being efficient for survival in any situation, but every time I have witnessed a class in which this is taught, body armor is nonexistent. The truth is that all the "coolness" goes away when you teach ground fighting with body armor. Simplicity becomes an unavoidable necessity. Without simplicity, techniques won't work, and practitioners will find themselves quickly drained of energy.

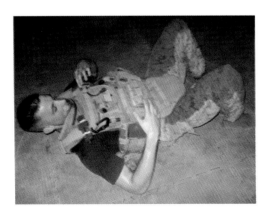 

Let me state the obvious: walking with body armor is more difficult than walking without it. The same is true of ground fighting with body armor. However, let's review this analogy of walking and ground fighting with body armor more in-depth.

The average human spends more than three-fourths of the day standing, sitting, or walking. The position in which the average human spends the least amount of time is lying down, and that is usually for sleeping, relaxing and watching television on the couch. Thus, over the course of one's life, the mind and the muscles relate being upright to activity and the use of energy. Lying down in a ground-oriented position becomes related to rest and conservation of energy. So, just by living, the body becomes efficient at using energy when upright, and activities done while upright are usually easier for the body to do than activities while lying down.

Consider someone who has finished an exhausting activity; the first thing they usually want to do is lie down. Depending on the situation, they will sit down if necessary, but if they could lie down, they probably would. Because the body correlates lying down to being at a state of rest, it is a shock to the body when this position becomes a position of activity. Therefore, the body uses more energy to perform movements from this position than it does from upright positions.

Try this out! Go into a private room and lie on the ground, and then get up quickly. Do this four times and you will notice an increase (slight or extreme, depending on your cardiovascular conditioning) in your breathing. Try walking from one end of the room and back three times, then check your breathing (or, if you are a nut like me, check your heart rate). Then roll or crawl from one end of the room to the other three times and check your breathing (or pulse). You will most likely notice an increase in your rate of breath or pulse.

This is why even someone in good physical condition will become exhausted shortly after starting ground fighting. Now if one adds the bulk and weight of body armor along with the weight and strength of a opponent to this natural rest position, the body really goes through a shock. It not only has to adjust to the new weight, but also a new way of moving because of the restriction of movement, combined with a life and death struggle.

Are you getting the picture yet? I have seen and learned some cool things in ground fighting, but those same cool things aren't that easy to accomplish in the battlefield, and they are definitely not that efficient. Any real combative system claiming to prepare a service member for the battlefield should be aware of, and teach its practitioners about this.

WHAT IS B.G.C.?

"On the field of battle man is not only a thinking animal, he is a beast of burden. He is given great weights to carry. But unlike the mule, the jeep, or any other carrier, his chief function in war does not begin until the time he delivers that burden to the appointed ground... In fact we have always done better by a mule than by a man. We were careful not to load the mule with more than a third of his weight."

—S.L.A. Marshall, 1950

B.G.C. (Battlefield Ground Combat) is a means for a service member who has fallen to the ground, or been taken to the ground, to defend, incapacitate, or severely damage his adversary, rise to his or her feet, and continue the mission. Because it is created for the battlefield, B.G.C. always assumes that a weapon is involved in a ground altercation between a service member and an opponent. Thus, freedom of movement and limbs become more restricted than they would be in a non-battlefield encounter. When a weapon (such as knife, stick, or pistol) is involved, the paramount concern is keeping that blade from puncturing one's body, the stick from bludgeoning one into unconsciousness, or the pistol from firing a round into one's body. Therefore, making sure that the weapon is properly secured and kept in a non-threatening position is the first priority. To do this, at least one hand will be occupied controlling the weapon: misdirecting the weapon hand or holding it and trying to remove the weapon. Preferably two hands should be used for this, unless the other hand is reaching for your own weapon or causing damage to the enemy.

Occupying the hands in this fashion renders the use of certain ground fighting techniques ineffective or unsafe.

Another aspect that B.G.C. considers is the restriction of movement that the body armor creates. The locks and joint manipulations used in ground fighting become much more difficult, if not impossible, when the restriction of body armor hinders certain body movements or alignments.

In 2003, the U.S. Army Center for Army Lessons Learned published the findings of an assessment called *The Modern Warrior's Combat Load*. In this assessment, soldiers had two complaints about the body armor, which I shared as well:

- "The lack in freedom of arm movement. Soldiers stated that the I.B.A. often restricted their arm movement and caused their arms to go numb."
- "The lack of flexibility in SAPI Plates (strike plates). Soldiers noted how both plates were shaped the same yet since their back had a different formation than their chest they restricted movement and made them uncomfortable."

I remember the first time I fell while in my body armor. I immediately felt like a turtle on its back. My initial response was to roll to the left, get to my knees and stand up. It seemed as though it would be an easy task, but my first aid kit, which was attached to the outside of my left thigh, made it a little more difficult to accomplish than I expected. Rolling to the right was more difficult, because my pistol holster was attached to my right leg and my rifle was attached to the right side of my I.B.A. (body armor) It only took a few seconds for me to get up, but it was a much more difficult task than normal, not only because of the weight of the armor, but also because of the restricted movement and the additional, mandatory accessories.

As I said earlier, one has to create and train based on the operational realism of a service member's mission and equipment. The same ground fighting used for the arena may be usable in a detainee facility, but it becomes much less valid on the battlefield.

chapter 10

TECHNIQUE SET ONE

Through techniques comes the transmission of principles.
The "why" is more important than the "what." For if one knows
why something is done then adaptation becomes much easier.

PURPOSE

B.P.C. is dedicated to evolution and change. It is based on the full range of operational experiences. Thus, the plainclothes embassy soldier is taken into account, as well as the M.P. in garrison, and the infantryman in Iraq or Afghanistan. However, the battlefield armor-clad soldier is its primary focus, because this area has, for so long, been overlooked or not properly addressed by other systems.

The purpose of this chapter is to give the reader an abbreviated view of the B.P.C. Beginner Technique Set 1. Not all the techniques in this set are shown, because I didn't want the reader to look at the techniques and feel as though they could use these techniques in the real world without proper instruction. Furthermore, because this system was designed primarily for the American military combatant, it is important that the full dynamics of the techniques (as well as the curriculum) not be divulged in an open source fashion. The intent is to help conceal these tactics from those who would use them against the United States. This concealment will help to secure another advantage on the battlefield for the American service member trained in B.P.C.

EMPHASIS

In Technique Set 1, Phase 1 of B.P.C., emphasis is placed on quick defense and offense against uncontrolled gross motor attacks, as opposed to refined calculated attacks. The belief is that the chances of encountering an attacker or adversary that is highly trained in various weapons to such a skill level that, under duress, they will still be capable of using fine motor skills and strategically calculated strikes is low. Technique Set 1, Phase 1 is also important because the principles and technique basics taught in this set are the foundation upon which the rest of the system is built.

TECHNIQUES

When collecting or devising techniques for any battlefield combative system, there are primary focuses that should be addressed. Those focuses are: efficiency, effectiveness, and simplicity. When reviewing the techniques in this first set, even though they are presented in an abbreviated form, it will become quite apparent that the techniques adhere to these focuses.

Edged Weapon versus Edged Weapon

Edged Weapon versus Edged Weapon (Technique 1)

Note: In the modern application, the soldier transitions back to his primary weapon, clearing the malfunction or reloading, and then continuing mission.

(1) Attacker cuts from right to left.

(2) Defender avoids and moves to the outside of the attacker's body while cutting down on the attacker's arm.

(3) Defender delivers a finishing thrust to the throat.

(4) Defender reassumes battle position and continues battle.

Edged Weapon versus Edged Weapon (Technique 2)

Note: In the modern application, the soldier transitions back to his primary weapon, clearing the malfunction or reloading and then continuing mission.

(1) Attacker cuts from left to right.

(2) Defender avoids and moves to the inside of the attacker's body while cutting down on the attacker's arm.

(3) Defender delivers a finishing thrust/slash to the throat.

(4) Defender reassumes battle position and continues battle.

Edged Weapon versus Edged Weapon (Technique 3)

Note: In the modern application, the soldier transitions back to his primary weapon, clearing the malfunction or reloading, and then continuing the mission.

(1) Attacker stabs downward.

(2) Defender avoids and moves to the outside of the attacker's body while cutting down on the attacker's arm.

(3) Defender delivers a finishing thrust to the throat.

(4) Defender reassumes battle position and continues battle.

Edged Weapon versus Edged Weapon (Technique 4)

Note: In the modern application, the soldier transitions back to his primary weapon, clearing the malfunction or reloading, and then continuing mission.

(1) Attacker stabs downward.

(2) Defender avoids and moves to the inside of the attacker's body while cutting down on the attacker's arm.

(3) Defender delivers a finishing thrust to the throat.

(4) Defender reassumes battle position and continues battle.

Edged Weapon versus Edged Weapon (Technique 5)

Note: In the modern application, the soldier transitions back to his primary weapon, clearing the malfunction or reloading, and then continuing mission.

(1) Attacker stabs upward/inward.

(2) Defender avoids and moves to the inside of the attacker's body while counterattacking attacker's arm.

(3) Defender delivers a finishing thrust to the throat or body.

(4) Defender reassumes battle position and continues battle.

Edged Weapon versus Edged Weapon (Technique 6)

Note: In the modern application, the soldier transitions back to his primary weapon, clearing the malfunction or reloading and then continuing mission.

(1) Attacker stabs upward/inward.

(2) Defender avoids and moves to the inside of the attacker's body while counterattacking the attackers arm.

(3) Defender delivers a finishing thrust to the throat or body.

(4) Defender reassumes battle position and continues battle.

Pistol versus Edged Weapon

Pistol versus Edged Weapon (Technique 1)

(1) Weapon malfunctions or runs dry during direct or defensive action.

(2) Before the defender can transition or reload, the attacker cuts from right to left.
Defender avoids strike, moving to the outside of the attacker's body.

(3) Defender secures attacking arm, and counterstrikes.

(4) Defender strikes collar/neck and spirals the attacker to the ground.

(5) Defender strikes the attacker's face with weapon.

(6) Defender delivers a final, incapacitating stomp on the face.

(7) Defender clears malfunction, reloads or transitions to secondary weapon, reassumes battle position, and continues battle.

Pistol versus Edged Weapon (Technique 2)

(1) Weapon malfunctions or runs dry during direct or defensive action.

(2) Before the defender can transition or reload, the attacker cuts from left to right.
Defender avoids strike, moving to the inside of the attacker's body.

(3) Defender secures attacking arm, and counterstrikes.

(4) Defender strikes collar/neck and spirals the attacker to the ground.

(5) Defender strikes the attacker's face with weapon.

(6) Defender delivers a final, incapacitating stomp on the face.

(7) Defender clears malfunction, reloads or transitions to secondary weapon, reassumes battle position, and continues battle.

Pistol versus Edged Weapon (Technique 3)

(1) Weapon malfunctions or runs dry during direct or defensive action.

(2) Before the defender can transition or reload, the attacker stabs downward. Defender avoids strike, moving to the outside of the attacker's body.

(3) Defender secures attacking arm, and counterstrikes.

(4) Defender strikes collar/neck and spirals the attacker to the ground.

(5) Defender strikes the attacker's face with weapon.

(6) Defender delivers a final, incapacitating stomp on the face.

(7) Defender clears malfunction, reloads or transitions to secondary weapon, reassumes battle position, and continues battle.

Pistol versus Edged Weapon (Technique 4)

(1) Weapon malfunctions or runs dry during direct or defensive action.

(2) Before the defender can transition or reload, the attacker stabs downward.
Defender avoids strike, moving to the inside of the attacker's body.

(3) Defender secures attacking arm, and counterstrikes.

(4) Defender strikes collar/neck and spirals the attacker to the ground.

(5) Defender strikes the attacker's face with weapon.

(6) Defender delivers a final, incapacitating stomp on the face.

(7) Defender clears malfunction, reloads or transitions to secondary weapon, reassumes battle position, and continues battle.

Pistol versus Edged Weapon (Technique 5)

(1) Weapon malfunctions or runs dry during direct or defensive action.

(2) Before the defender can transition or reload, the attacker stabs downward.
Defender avoids strike, moving to the inside of the attacker's body.

(3) Defender secures attacking arm, and counterstrikes.

(4) Defender strikes collar/neck and spirals the attacker to the ground.

(5) Defender strikes the attacker's face with weapon.

(6) Defender delivers a final, incapacitating stomp on the face.

(7) Defender clears malfunction, reloads or transitions to secondary weapon,
reassumes battle position, and continues battle.

Pistol versus Edged Weapon (Technique 6)

(1) Weapon malfunctions or runs dry during direct or defensive action.

(2) Before the defender can transition or reload, the attacker stabs downward.
Defender avoids strike, moving to the inside of the attacker's body.

(3) Defender secures attacking arm and counterstrikes.

(4) Defender strikes collar/neck and spirals the attacker to the ground.

(5) Defender strikes the attacker's face with weapon.

(6) Defender delivers a final, incapacitating stomp on the face.

(7) Defender clears malfunction, reloads or transitions to secondary weapon,
reassumes battle position, and continues battle.

Battlefield Ground Combat

Combat Grappling (Technique 1)

(1) Attacker stabs downward into chest/neck from a right-side kneeling position.

(2) Defender secures the attacker's wrist to stop thrust and kick right leg towards left side.

(3) Defender rolls his body to the left guiding the attacker's right elbow over his head.

(4) Defender brings his knees under him, while controlling knife hand and pinning the attacker's shoulder to the ground.

(5) Defender places left knee on attacker's back, and smashes his head into the ground.

(6) Defender removes attacker's knife, delivers a final, incapacitating blow, reassumes standing battle position, and continues mission.

Combat Grappling (Technique 2)

(1) Attacker stabs downward into chest/neck from a right-side kneeling position.

(2) Defender secures the attacker's wrist to stop thrust and wedges right knee between himself and the attacker.

(3) Defender brings left leg up and kicks to the right side of attacker's face.

(4) Defender uses the continual force of strike to rotate opponent to his back.

(5) Defender pulls back left foot and delivers a final incapacitating blow
(in the soldier's situation he pulls out his secondary weapon).

(6) Defender reassumes standing battle position and continues mission.

Combat Grappling (Technique 3)

(1) Attacker launches forward from a distance, stabbing downward into chest/neck.

(2) Defender kicks attacker's arm with right foot.

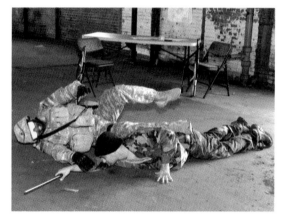

(3) Defender uses the continual force of the strike to force attacker's body to the ground.

(4) Defender rolls to the right.

(5) Defender swings left knee around to knee the attacker to the back of the head.

(6) Defender reassumes battle position and continues mission.

BONUS TECHNIQUES FROM VOLUME 2

Take down (Technique 1)

(1) Attacker grabs the muzzle of the defender's rifle.

(2) Defender steps behind attacker while simultaneously striking to the face with left palm and sweeping the attacker to the ground.

(3) Defender switches to his secondary weapon since attacker does not release his primary weapon.

(4) Defender reassumes battle position and continues mission.

Subject Control (Technique 1)

(1) Soldier approaches a surrendering enemy subject from an angle with weapon on target.

(2) Once just out of arm's reach, the soldier passes his rifle to the side and extends arms to guard and prepare to take control of the subject's head.

(3) Soldier shoots in and knees to the groin or midsection while simultaneously taking control of the subject's head.

(4) Soldier twists the subject's head; face moving counterclockwise.

(5) Soldier takes subject down to his back and kneels on him. When subject reaches out the soldier will grab at the wrist and elbow and pull the subject to his belly.

6) Soldier kneels on the subject's back and secures with restraints.

CONCLUSION

A Place For Everything

Everything has its place, but in finding that place one has to truly look at the operational environment, and the operational realism needed for the place in which they are trying to operate.

To me, this phrase sums up my point of view on military combatives. Contrary to what you might think, this book is not a way of saying "my system is better than yours." The purpose of this book is to inform the reader about B.P.C., the theories behind its creation, and why it is valid. The systems currently taught in the military have some valid points and teachings. However, they often lack efficient and effective application for armored combat on the battlefield. Therefore, the use of principles from an art that was designed for armored combat will be much more applicable for armored combatants than an art that was not created for such a scenario.

I hope that my brave countrymen and countrywomen, who volunteered to fight for our wonderful nation, understand my theories and have gained a better insight on the subject of battlefield combatives from this book.

DEDICATION & AFTER ACTION REVIEWS

This book is dedicated to all my hard-working, awesome, and inspiring practitioners that took time out of their busy mission schedules to train vigorously for hours in B.P.C. while on deployment in Iraq.

As a member of the special operations community for 12 years, I have commanded several unique organizations with a variety of missions. Over the years, I have come to realize that combative training is a key ingredient in the making of a special ops individual. The special operations community employs a variety of combative training systems. The recent evolution of the Battlefield Proximity Combat system captures the essence of all the others, but incorporates new techniques against an evolving threat of the 21st century. I have personally observed Hakim Isler teach his system to my soldiers operating in the toughest parts of Ramadi, Iraq. The confidence with which these soldiers were able to operate on the forward edge of the battlefield always paid dividends.

Michael Layrisson
LTC, USA

Battlefield Proximity Combat (B.P.C.) system offers an ideal program for military members. No other combative program I've seen fully integrates all environments found on today's battlefield. B.P.C. uses a simple, progressive training system based on functional movements that are repeated throughout the course. The repetition of these movements program "muscle memory" into participants, allowing graduates near instantaneous response to situations they are likely to encounter on today's battlefield. B.P.C. addresses many shortcomings of the Army's combative program, such as fighting in full body armor. Any service member that completes this program will have a distinct advantage on the battlefield.

Robert Schoenenberger
CPT, USA

❋　　❋　　❋　　❋　　❋

The Battlefield Proximity Combat system is easy for soldiers to train and master in a sufficient period of time. Its simplicity is suitable for the high stress environment of combat where mass confusion often afford soldiers little time to think. They must rely on learned instinct, which is why B.P.C. will give those who train in it a great chance of survival.

Dat T. Nguyen
CPT, AR

❋　　❋　　❋　　❋　　❋

B.P.C. is the simplest, yet effective, combative system that I have studied. B.P.C., to me, is a system I see more useful for the present-day combat soldier than the current combative system that I was trained through the Army. All fighting systems have their place, depending upon the given time and situation. B.P.C.'s time and place is here, and the situation is where our combat soldiers of today may or will find themselves.

Toland O. Agee
SSG, USA

❋　　❋　　❋　　❋　　❋

The B.P.C. system is a remarkably easy system that is perfect for today's soldier. He teaches basic skills in unarmed combat as it relates to situations that soldiers of today may find themselves. He incorporates simplicity, violence of action, and ease of movement into the system enabling the soldier to fight and win in today's combat.

Joshua S. Dillinger
SSG, AR

❊ ❊ ❊ ❊ ❊

The training I've received through B.P.C. has given me the advantage I'll need when my life is in danger. I've also gained the confidence necessary to make use of that advantage when death or serious injury is at stake. With my training in Battlefield Proximity Combat, I now feel better prepared to handle a hand-to-hand combat engagement, as well as the dangerous situations of everyday life.

Justin Bibee
USMC

❊ ❊ ❊ ❊ ❊

B.P.C. is new, an up-to-date in the military battlefield fighting system. I like the idea of a combative system designed for the general military members regardless of their skill. It not only teaches you the moves of how to defend yourself when you have a weapons malfunction in full battle armor, it also teaches you up-right and ground fighting styles to possibly save your life in combat. Through the three phases, I have learned how to protect my vitals and to counter the enemy's initial engagement with and without gear on. I also like the fact that we learn a little bit about the samurai and how B.P.C. is based on past principles revolutionized and brought to today's fighting standards.

Seth Knowles
USMC

❊ ❊ ❊ ❊ ❊

I have taken a number of different combative classes since joining the U.S. Army. Each one is good in its own way, but Battlefield Proximity Combat stands above the rest. Hakim Isler has developed a much more modern and effective program for combative training. B.P.C. focuses on real life scenarios for real combat. Hakim is an excellent instructor with an array of knowledge, which he pours into this program. Since taking this class, I am much more confident in my skills with an array of weapons. Every soldier, marine, sailor, and airman should be afforded the chance to learn the skills that Hakim Isler brings to the table.

Brian Whittle
SGT, USA

❋   ❋   ❋   ❋   ❋

I found Battlefield Proximity Combat to be a vast improvement over current military hand-to-hand combat fighting systems. He has used his expertise to devise a system of fighting specially geared to deal with current real-world combat situations, yet it is flexible enough to be used for years to come. As a non-commissioned officer, I feel that my soldiers will greatly benefit from learning B.P.C., both in their ability to face and defeat enemies in combat, and in their understanding of the warrior spirit. In the future, I would like to see Battlefield Proximity Combat adopted by the Department of Defense as a military-wide system for hand-to-hand combat.

Robert N. Green
SGT, USA

❋   ❋   ❋   ❋   ❋

Battlefield Proximity Combat is a system designed for military by military. B.P.C. combines lethal weapons techniques, defensive and offensive movements, and grappling for the battlefield, into a concise yet simple close quarters combat system. Having learned these techniques, I feel more confident in my fighting abilities, and more confident in myself as a soldier.

Richard L. Skinner III
SPC, USA

ACKNOWLEDGEMENTS

I would also like to give a special thanks to:
Stephen K. Hayes – for his training and guidance as my friend and teacher
Toland Omar Agee – for his unwavering friendship and loyalty
Hardee Merritt – for his friendship and help in completing this project
Rachael Santillan – for her amazing photographic and artistic talents
Brian Dukes – for using his amazing editing skill on the first draft of this manuscript.

For more information go to: bpccombatives.com